CRYSTAL MAGIC

WELBECK
CHILDREN'S BOOKS

First published in the USA in 2024
by Welbeck Children's Books
An imprint of Hachette Children's Group

10 9 8 7 6 5 4 3 2 1

ISBN: 978 1 80453 661 2

Printed in Dongguan, China

Welbeck Children's Books
An imprint of Hachette Children's Group
Part of Hodder & Stoughton Limited
Carmelite House, 50 Victoria Embankment
London EC4Y 0DZ
An Hachette UK Company
www.hachette.co.uk
www.hachettechildrens.co.uk

The publishers would like to thank the following sources for their kind permission to reproduce the pictures in this book.

ALAMY: ZUMA Press, Inc. 68. GETTY IMAGES: filo 26-27C. SHUTTERSTOCK: Alexei A 29T; Malysh A 29B; Africa Studio 17T; Arkhipov Aleksey 54; Yurkina Alexandra all images 16-17 apart from 17T; Fernando Astasio Avila 25T; Babin 15BR; Mehmet Gokhan Bayhan 39T; Billion Photos 35BR; BOOCYS 9BR; bkkillustrator 44; Cartoonzone 12; Cast Of Thousands 46; DenisNata 21BR; DFree 67BR; FamStudio 35T; Finesell 5CLB, 15T; FotoMirta 6-7C; GaleanoFotografo 50-51C, 70TCL; Ground Picture 55R; Ilizia 21TR; Imfoto 10-11BC, 48-49CT, 70BCL, 71CR; Eric Isselee 33; JaneMoon 45B, 71BCL; Sebastian Janicki 4TL, 4CLB, 4BL, 4BR, 5TR, 5BR, 14-15CB, 18-19C, 30-31CB, 32, 35BL, 42-43C, 70TR, 70CL, 71TCR, 71TR, 71FCR, 71BCL; ju_see 56; Ira Kalinicheva 19CR; KrimKate 4CR, 20-21C, 62, 70BCR; Vincent Lekabel 19TR; Winston Link 41T; manfredxy 13, 71TL; Andrejs Marcenko 51B; Oliver Mohr 5CRA, 47BR; Svetlana Monyakova 9TR; Mr SW Photo 40CR; muratart 53B; nadisja 66TR, 66CR; NPDstock 51T; NickKnight 4CLA, 31T; olpo 52-53C, 71BR; J.Palys 5BL, 47TR; J. Paredes 43B; PeopleImages.com – Yuri A 6BL; Pixfiction 39B; PNSJ88 63L, 71BL; pukach 49B; Red Umbrella and Donkey 11TR; Reload Design 8-9C, 70BR; Birgith Roosipuu 66B; Minakryn Rusian 4TR, 40-41C, 55L, 59L, 70TL, 70CR, 70BL; Albert Russ 64-65C, 71CL; Roman Samborskyi 61B; Victoria Shapiro 61T; Smart Calendar 22-23C, 70TCR; snova.mir 7BR; Tarzhanova 59R; Tinseltown 67BC; toey19863 23BR; 220 Selfmade studio 23TR; Valentyn Volkov 65R; vvoe 5TL, 5CLA, 5CR, 38-39C, 45T, 47CR, 47CRB, 60-61C, 71TCL, 71FCL; Wirestock Creators 4CL, 24-25CB, 69, 70FCR; Bjoern Wylezich 5CRB, 28-29C, 70FCL; Irina Zharkova31 31B; Zoomik 63R. Graphic elements from GETTY IMAGES: Sudowoodo; hellokisdittur.

Every effort has been made to acknowledge correctly and contact the source and/or copyright holder of each picture. Any unintentional errors or omissions will be corrected in future editions of this book.

CRYSTAL MAGIC

DISCOVER THE SECRET
WORLD OF CRYSTALS

CONTENTS

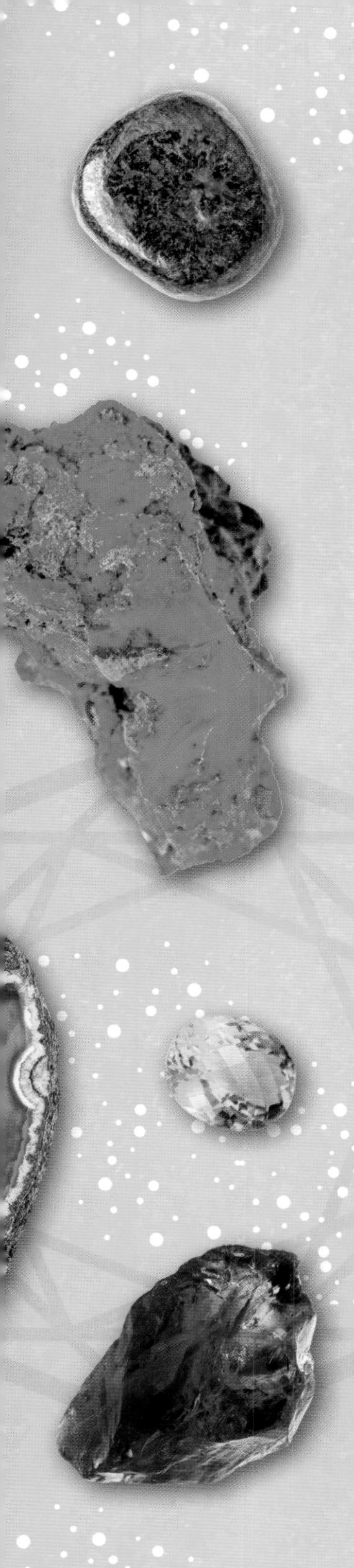

Welcome

Inside this book, you'll find everything you need to know about the fascinating world of crystals, gemstones, and minerals.

By opening your mind to the power of possibility and turning to nature, you too can harness the wonder of crystals. Whether you're looking for a crystal to bring you luck or to help with poor sleep, this guide has the answers.

Harness the power of crystals as you discover this gentle and natural approach to nourishment, healing, and wellbeing.

Introducing crystals into your lifestyle can empower you to take back control of your life and put your health and happiness first. So, what are you waiting for? Your journey to contentment starts here . . .

CRYSTAL FACT

Did you know that putting pressure on certain crystals creates electricity? This was discovered in 1880 by French physicist Pierre Curie. His scientific findings support the idea that crystals can affect our minds and bodies.

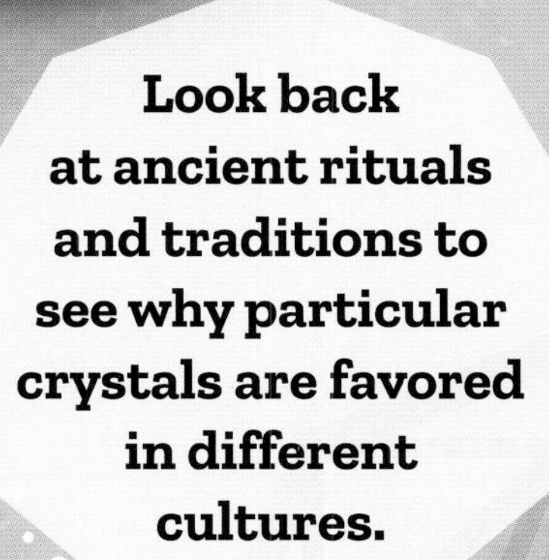

CRYSTAL, MINERAL, OR ROCK?

Mineral

This is a natural material made up of only one substance. Minerals form many things including crystals, rocks, pebbles, or sand.

Crystal

All crystals are made from minerals, but not all minerals are crystals. Each individual crystal is made up of one mineral. To be classified as a crystal, it must be one of seven specific shapes.

Rock

A rock can be made from more than one type of mineral, and it's not one of the seven crystal shapes.

Rose QUARTZ

This rosy-hued crystal is a gem that inspires warmth, friendship, and love.

COLOR: **Pink**

Rose quartz crystals are a very pale, milky pink.

GOOD FOR: **The heart**

Rose quartz is a favorite for those seeking a crystal to bring love and friendship.

UNCONDITIONAL LOVE

If you're looking to start new friendships, or you just want to make the ones you have even better, then hold onto this stone. This gem brings unconditional love, friendship, and attraction.

WARM EMBRACE

Rose quartz is known as a mothering crystal and is loved by those looking for comfort and reassurance as well as wisdom. To channel all the good stuff, try placing the gem on your chest or at the base of your spine.

ANCIENT TIMES

People have been enjoying the magical powers of rose quartz for a long, long time. In fact, the Egyptians thought it could eliminate wrinkles and halt aging. No wonder it has been found in stone masks and jewelry uncovered in their tombs.

SOAK IT UP

Add some umph to your self-care routine by popping rose quartz into your bath. Bathing with this crystal welcomes warmth and protection, plus it encourages self-love.

AS YOU SLEEP

If you're feeling like life is busy and it's hard to find your inner peace, give this a try. Simply place a rose quartz gem near your bed while you sleep to bring harmony back into your life.

Sapphire

A stone of wisdom and prosperity, sapphire is thought to bring about spiritual enlightenment and attract gifts of all kinds.

COLOR: Blue

Sapphire is most commonly blue, but it can come in a variety of colors, including yellow, pink, and even black.

GOOD FOR:

The mind (and the purse!)

Those seeking answers and financial abundance may benefit from this stone.

RARE FIND

Of all the shades of sapphire, medium-deep cornflower blue is the most prized. This is because it is extremely rare to find a sapphire of such pure blue. However, that doesn't mean other color varieties don't have value—each has its unique benefits. For example, midnight blue enhances intuition, purple promotes spiritual growth, and yellow is believed to attract good fortune.

IN HISTORY

Those using this stone for guidance are in good company. Ancient Greeks were known to wear sapphire when seeking answers from the Oracle, while Buddhists and Hindus used it during worship.

FIT FOR A QUEEN

Sapphire has long been connected to nobility and is a firm favorite with kings and queens. Queen Victoria loved the stone, and Princess Diana's 12-carat Ceylon sapphire and diamond ring is perhaps the most famous engagement ring in the world.

TRUE TREASURE

Everyone wants a piece of sapphire. In 1964, a highly prized sapphire named The Star of India was famously stolen from the American Museum of Natural History. The 563.35-carat sapphire, which is the largest of its kind in the world, has stars on both of its sides and an elusive past shrouded in mystery and mythology. Fortunately, it was recovered years later.

AS JEWELRY

Blue sapphire stimulates the throat chakra, which plays an essential role in communication and self-expression. To make the best use of this property, wear the stone around your neck so that it is in active contact with the throat.

Aventurine

Known as the stone of opportunity, aventurine is believed to bring good luck, prosperity, and courage.

LUCKY DISCOVERY

Aventurine comes from the Italian word "avventura," which means "by chance." This is both a nod to the good fortune the stone can offer and a reference to how it was discovered by mistake in the 18th century by glass workers in Italy.

COLOR: **Green**

Aventurine is most commonly green, but other color varieties exist, including blue, orange, and yellow.

GOOD FOR: **Self-esteem**

If it's confidence and a lucky break you're after, aventurine is the stone for you.

WARRIOR ENERGY

Before this stone was sold in shops, it guarded the shields of Amazon warrior queens, and for centuries, was even known as the "stone of the Amazons." Use it to face battles of your own or look to it for protection. Aventurine has your back.

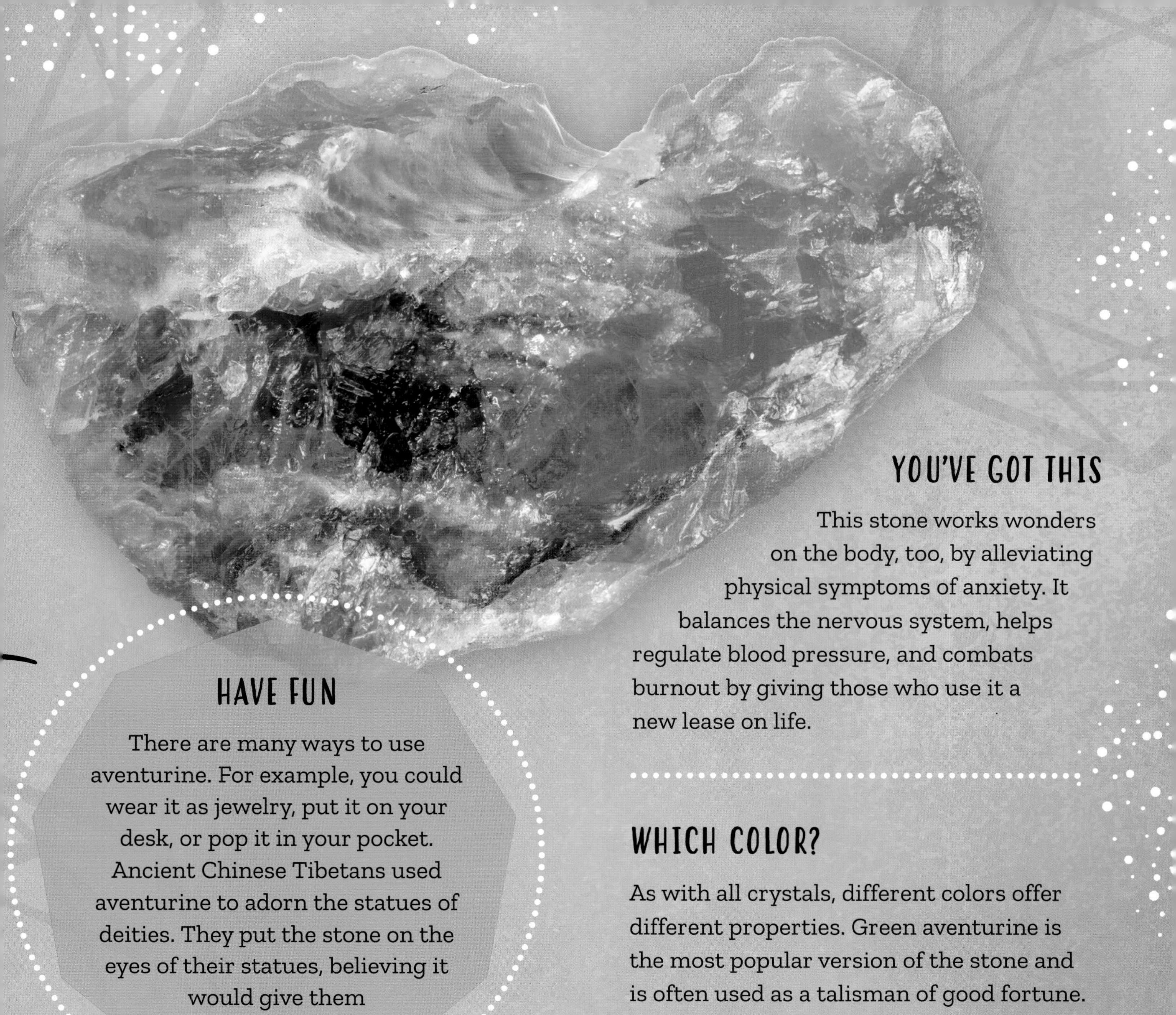

YOU'VE GOT THIS

This stone works wonders on the body, too, by alleviating physical symptoms of anxiety. It balances the nervous system, helps regulate blood pressure, and combats burnout by giving those who use it a new lease on life.

HAVE FUN

There are many ways to use aventurine. For example, you could wear it as jewelry, put it on your desk, or pop it in your pocket. Ancient Chinese Tibetans used aventurine to adorn the statues of deities. They put the stone on the eyes of their statues, believing it would give them visionary powers.

WHICH COLOR?

As with all crystals, different colors offer different properties. Green aventurine is the most popular version of the stone and is often used as a talisman of good fortune. On the other hand, blue aventurine helps with spiritual guidance, and red aventurine embodies life-force energy.

Citrine

Nicknamed the "merchant stone," citrine is thought to attract wealth and success, and inspire creativity.

COLOR: **Golden yellow**

Citrine is most commonly golden yellow in color, but its shade can vary from pale yellow to brownish red.

GOOD FOR: **Creativity**

Struggling creatives may find inspiration with this stone, and potentially even success.

POWER AND PASSION

Citrine stimulates the solar plexus chakra and sacral chakra, making it an all-around great crystal for any struggling creatives. The solar plexus is where we gain strength and power, and the sacral chakra is responsible for passion and creativity.

BRIGHT ORIGINS

The name citrine comes from the Old French word for lemon, referring to the crystal's wonderfully vibrant color. Before 1556, citrine was simply known as yellow quartz. Now it goes by several names, including the "merchant's stone," "the money stone," and "the sunshine stone."

EMPERORS' CHOICE

If it's wealth and success you're after, citrine is a good choice. In ancient Chinese society, citrine was seen as the "success stone" because it was thought to bring good fortune to the wearer. Chinese emperors wore it for that reason, and to increase their intellectual abilities.

A TIMELESS GEM

This radiant stone has been cherished by high-profile figures for centuries. Queen Victoria, whose reign defined the Victorian era, and Greta Garbo, a 1930s Hollywood icon, are two celebs who famously wore citrine and helped make it popular.

POCKETFUL OF SUNSHINE

Brimming with warm energy, it's no wonder that citrine is so closely linked to the Sun. In ancient times, the Greeks and Romans thought the stone carried the power of the Sun god and used it for energy and protection. In modern times, it is used in a similar way, as a pick-me-up on dark days.

WHICH ELEMENT ARE YOU?

Everyone has a birthstone, just like everyone has a star sign. The stone you have depends on the month when you were born. Find yours below to see what it means!

Month:
January
Stone:
Garnet
Meaning:
Protection

Month:
February
Stone:
Amethyst
Meaning:
Contentment

Month:
March
Stone:
Aquamarine
Meaning:
Serenity

Month:
July
Stone:
Ruby
Meaning:
Passion

Month:
August
Stone:
Peridot
Meaning:
Beauty

Month:
September
Stone:
Sapphire
Meaning:
Wisdom

DID YOU KNOW?

Wearing your birthstone is supposed to bring you luck and protection.

UNBREAKABLE

Diamonds are super strong, which is why they are used in rings to symbolize unbreakable love.

Month:
April
Stone:
Diamond
Meaning:
Strength

Month:
May
Stone:
Emerald
Meaning:
Growth

Month:
June
Stone:
Pearl
Meaning:
Love

STONE OF MYSTERY

For centuries, pearls were seen as mega mysterious—nobody could figure out where they came from. In China, they believed pearls came from a dragon's brain, but they actually come from oysters!

Month:
October
Stone:
Opal
Meaning:
Healing

Month:
November
Stone:
Topaz
Meaning:
Confidence

Month:
December
Stone:
Turquoise
Meaning:
Friendship

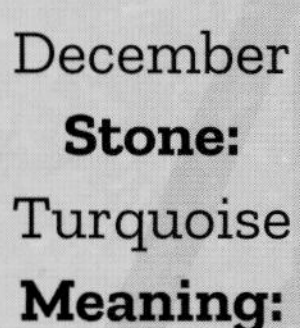

Lapis LAZULI

A stone of wisdom and truth, lapis lazuli is believed to stimulate psychic abilities and bring enlightenment.

COLOR: **Blue**

Lapis lazuli is an intense deep blue color that sometimes includes golden flakes of pyrite.

GOOD FOR: **Self-expression**

Those feeling lost or inhibited may find freedom with this empowering stone.

BE ENLIGHTENED

This stone is good for clearing blockages in the throat chakra and third eye chakra, helping you to feel confident and connected with your higher self. The throat chakra is linked to self-expression and inner truth, whereas the third eye chakra is considered the gateway to spiritual enlightenment.

COOL LIKE CLEOPATRA

Some used the stone as makeup to express themselves. In ancient Egypt, it was fashionable to wear ground lapis lazuli as eyeshadow. Egyptian queen and beauty icon Cleopatra herself used the blue pigment to create her signature eye makeup look.

ARTISTIC ROOTS

Lapis lazuli fueled the creative expression of past artists. In the Middle Ages, painters ground it up to make the deep blue pigment named ultramarine, and Michelangelo even used it to paint the Sistine Chapel. This blue pigment was so precious, it cost more than gold!

PRETTIER THAN POETRY

Lapis lazuli is more than just a pretty stone. With its deep blue coloring and golden flecks, it has long evoked comparisons to the starry sky and is thought to encompass the truth of the cosmos. No wonder poets are so enthralled by it!

SWEET DREAMS

Lapis lazuli has a host of physical benefits, including purifying the blood, soothing areas of inflammation, and alleviating insomnia. To get an extra good night's sleep, place the stone under your pillow and be prepared for some insightful, lucid dreams.

Rhodonite

A stone of love and tenderness, rhodonite helps break down emotional barriers and offers comfort and protection.

COLOR: **Pink**

Rhodonite derives from the Greek word "rhodos," meaning rose, and ranges from light pink to deep red in color.

GOOD FOR: **The heart**

Look to this crystal to cultivate love and compassion, and heal emotional wounds.

GOODBYE NEGATIVITY

During the healing process, rhodonite is thought to absorb negative energy. To keep the stone fresh and active, it is a good idea to clean it every now and then with a soft brush and warm, soapy water.

RHODONITE AND RUSSIA

Russia loves rhodonite. Historically, Russian carvers used the stone for all sorts of things, including as a protective talisman. Parents would place it in their babies' cribs to help them become strong and free like eagles, which, according to legend, stored rhodonite in their nests. Today, Russian children exchange rhodonite eggs on Easter to express love and affection.

KEEP IT CLOSE

Unlike some other crystals in this book, rhodonite is easily mined and accessible. Though its monetary value isn't high, rhodonite is still highly prized for its metaphysical value as a stone of love and protection. Wear it as jewelry to carry its gifts with you.

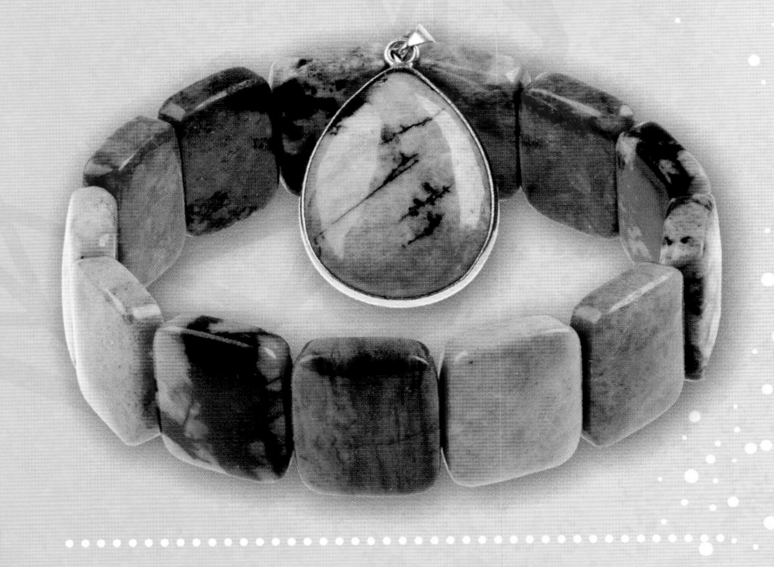

LOVE YOURSELF

This crystal is deeply connected to the heart chakra, which is the energetic center for love, compassion, empathy, and forgiveness. Consequently, Rhodonite can help with healing emotional scars.

HAPPY HEART

Rhodonite is said to have great physical healing properties, too. It can take the sting out of insect bites, heal wounds, and reduce scarring. It is also thought to help with heart palpitations and improve blood circulation.

Jade

This generous green stone guides us toward wealth and good relationships.

COLOR: **Green**

Jade comes in different colors, but green is the most iconic.

GOOD FOR: **Luck**

This protective stone brings good fortune and friendship.

LUCKY CHARM

As a bringer of good luck, jade is sometimes placed around people's homes to encourage the flow of positive energy. Jade is also cherished for is its associations with purity and harmony.

SKIN CARE

Jade rollers have been a key part of Chinese skincare regimes since as far back as the 7th century. Why jade? It's believed to boost circulation and reduce skin puffiness. Try this at home by putting your jade in the fridge and using it to soothe and cool tired skin.

JUST DREAMY

Jade is known as a dream stone. The stone can be used as a tool in dream-work when trying to channel psychic abilities or connect with spirit guides. Pop your jade under your pillow as you snooze to experience crystal clear dreams.

MYSTICAL MAGIC

Jade has been celebrated around the world for thousands of years. In New Zealand's Māori culture, jade is known as "taonga," which means "treasure." But nowhere in the world loves joyous jade more than China. The stone is a major part of Chinese culture and appears etched into jewelry and statues. Bangles made from jade are worn for protection.

HEALING

Beyond its spiritual benefits, jade is used by those suffering from issues with their kidneys and adrenal glands. Many believe that jade helps these organs heal from toxins. In fact, the name "jade" comes from the Spanish "piedra de ijada," which means "stone for the pain in the side."

Apophyllite

This white stone eases anxiety to make room for logic while restoring inner peace.

COLOR: **White**

Apophyllite usually has an icy or snow-like appearance.

GOOD FOR:

Psychic powers

If you can open your mind, this stone could be a gateway to the wider spiritual world.

THE TRUTH

By opening the third eye chakra, this shimmering stone helps you to see into the past and the future. Not only that, but it helps you to see more clearly so you're able to identify the truth no matter what.

SELF CARE

Take a few minutes out of your day to meditate with this stone by holding it in the palms of your hands. This simple ritual will foster patience and help you find a sense of calm. What's more, it will encourage you to practice self-love.

SPIRITUAL WISDOM

This bright white crystal opens the third eye chakra—the center for intuition and spiritual wisdom. It helps you to access past life experiences and to gain deeper insight. Some even say it helps people connect with angels!

CHARGED UP

Apophyllite is closely linked to the Moon, and that's where it gets its energy. With that in mind, you can charge up your apophyllite under the light of a full moon or new moon. Another way to recharge apophyllite is by burying the stone in soil—which also gets rid of any negative energy that's built up inside.

ANCIENT TIMES

Traditionally, Hindus would pass mirror apophyllite (a high-quality and clear version of apophyllite) down to younger generations in their family as a mirror to the past. They could then gaze into the stone to learn from the good and bad in their family's history. In Chinese Tibetan culture, however, apophyllite would be used to help with breathing-related issues, such as asthma, as well as with allergies.

CHAKRAS

You might hear us talk a lot about chakras in this book, and there's a good reason for that! In Hinduism and Buddhism, chakras are the main energy centers in the body.

There are seven main chakras that run along the spine, starting with the crown chakra on the top of the head and ending with the root chakra in the tailbone area. Each chakra has its own associated color, organs, and specific meaning. When a chakra is blocked, it can affect our physical body, as well as our emotional and spiritual state. Therefore, it is important to understand the seven chakras to identify any problems and find the right crystal for you.

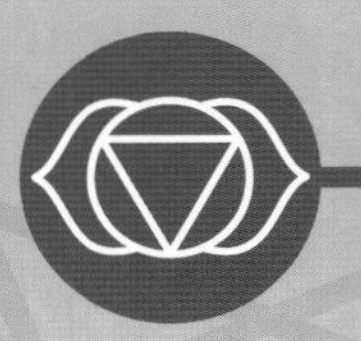

THIRD EYE CHAKRA
The chakra of intuition and imagination
Location: Between the eyes (it is also known as the "brow chakra")
Signs of block: Feeling out of touch with reality and experiencing headaches
Signs of balance: Being aware of your thoughts and knowing yourself well

HEART CHAKRA
The chakra of love and compassion
Location: The center of the chest, just above the heart
Signs of block: Feeling lonely or resentful and experiencing heart problems
Signs of balance: Having compassion, and giving and receiving love freely

SACRAL CHAKRA
The chakra of pleasure and creativity
Location: The lower abdomen
Signs of block: Lacking inspiration and feeling emotionally detached
Signs of balance: Feeling passionate and creatively fulfilled

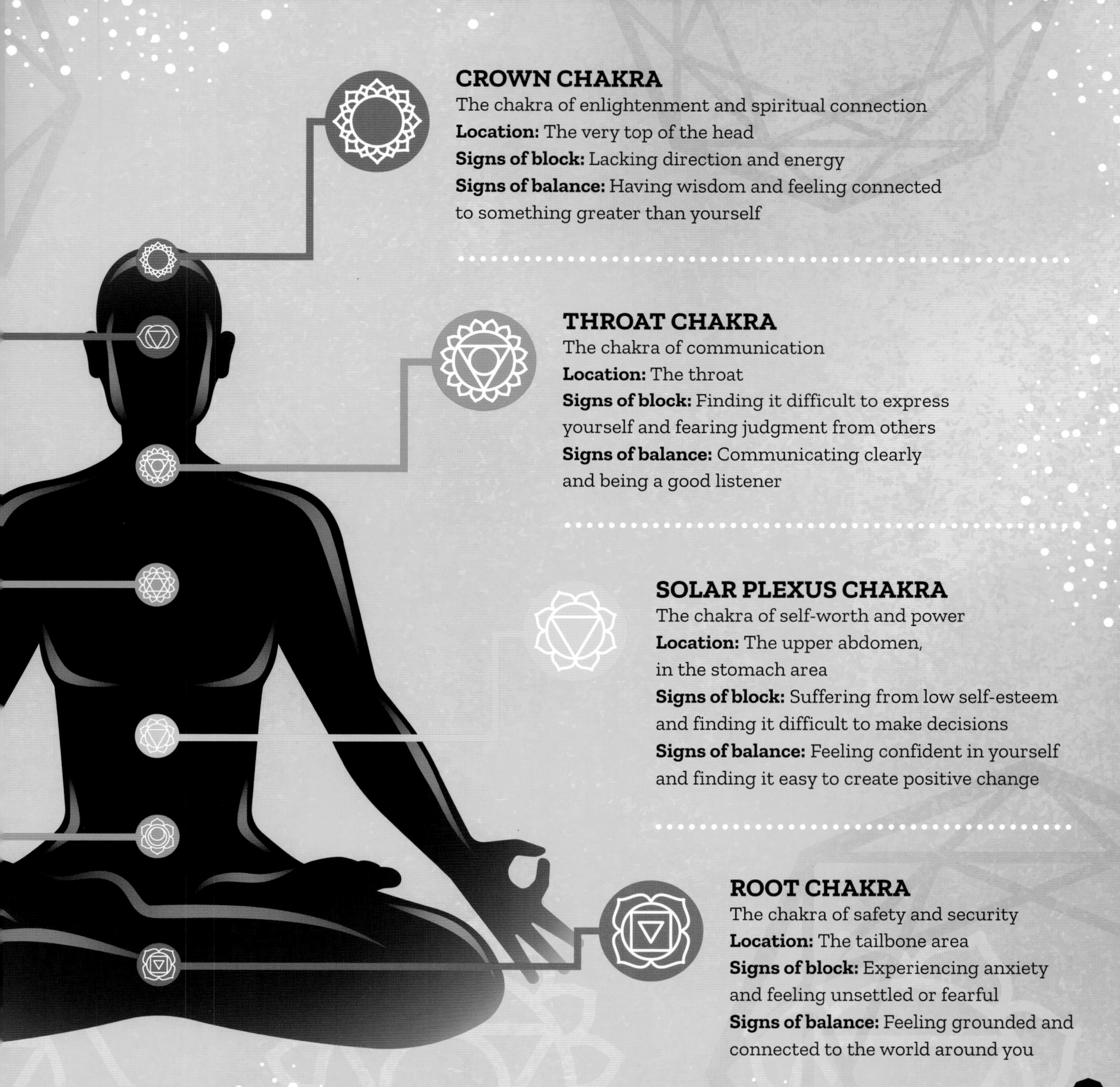

CROWN CHAKRA

The chakra of enlightenment and spiritual connection

Location: The very top of the head

Signs of block: Lacking direction and energy

Signs of balance: Having wisdom and feeling connected to something greater than yourself

THROAT CHAKRA

The chakra of communication

Location: The throat

Signs of block: Finding it difficult to express yourself and fearing judgment from others

Signs of balance: Communicating clearly and being a good listener

SOLAR PLEXUS CHAKRA

The chakra of self-worth and power

Location: The upper abdomen, in the stomach area

Signs of block: Suffering from low self-esteem and finding it difficult to make decisions

Signs of balance: Feeling confident in yourself and finding it easy to create positive change

ROOT CHAKRA

The chakra of safety and security

Location: The tailbone area

Signs of block: Experiencing anxiety and feeling unsettled or fearful

Signs of balance: Feeling grounded and connected to the world around you

Calcite

Turn to this stone to unite body, mind, and spirit for a higher spiritual connection.

COLOR:

Varied

Calcite can be many colors, including orange.

GOOD FOR:

Joints

It helps with arthritis and strengthens the skeleton.

SOUL SEARCHING

Calcite is renowned for its ability to activate chakras and prepare the body, mind, and spirit for higher spiritual connection. It nourishes the soul and cleanses away negative energy, making room for clear thinking.

HEALING

Calcite packs a punch when it comes to physical benefits. It detoxifies the organs so that they can function well. It also supports the skeletal system and keeps bones strong by balancing calcium in the body. Calcite helps the body absorb calcium. It can also break down calcification, which can contribute to arthritis.

PEACE

This crystal brings bright energy in abundance, helping with motivation and drive. So, if you're someone who finds yourself feeling down a lot, then calcite can help. It also encourages you to focus on what matters, while guiding you toward a more peaceful state of mind.

CALCITE CARE

Orange calcite loves a sun bath. Be mindful though, since it's a sensitive stone! Too many rays can mean calcite becomes brittle or fades—one to three hours is plenty. You can cleanse calcite with warm water and a soft cloth.

CREATIVE ENERGY

All colors of calcite are thought to enhance creative expression. When it comes to orange calcite, it is connected to the sacral chakra and is bursting with positive energy—a powerful combination for ensuring that creative ideas come to life.

Amethyst

This stone of spirituality and contentment brings calming vibes to clear the clutter.

CLEAR THE FOG

Racing minds that struggle to switch off can lead to exhaustion along with headaches, migraines, and eventual burnout. Those who struggle with brain fog or insomnia often turn to amethyst since this stone promotes sleep and rest!

COLOR:

Purple

Amethyst can be found in various tones from deep purple to lilac.

GOOD FOR:

The head

Amethyst is the perfect choice for those looking to calm a busy or worried mind.

SPIRITUAL CONTENTMENT

When life is busy, it can feel impossible to listen to your intuition as the noise of everyday life takes over. That's why this spiritual stone is so popular for meditation. It supports us in stepping back, reconnecting with ourselves, and tuning into our instincts.

GET A BOOST

Besides spiritual healing, amethyst is also a stone for physical wellness. It's believed to boost the immune system, making it easier to fend off infection and illness. With strong immunity, the body's power to heal greatly improves. It has a purifying nature that can help reduce stress and anxiety, too.

SACRED ENERGY CENTER

Amethyst is strongly linked with the crown chakra found at the top of the head—it's thought to restore balance and purpose. The crown chakra is the sacred energy center where we receive messages from the universe around us, and it connects the physical with the spiritual.

ROMANTIC LOVE

Amethyst is all about being open to love and forgiveness. Did you know that amethyst is the stone of Saint Valentine? The legend goes that the patron saint of romantic love wore an amethyst ring with Cupid carved into it.

Agate

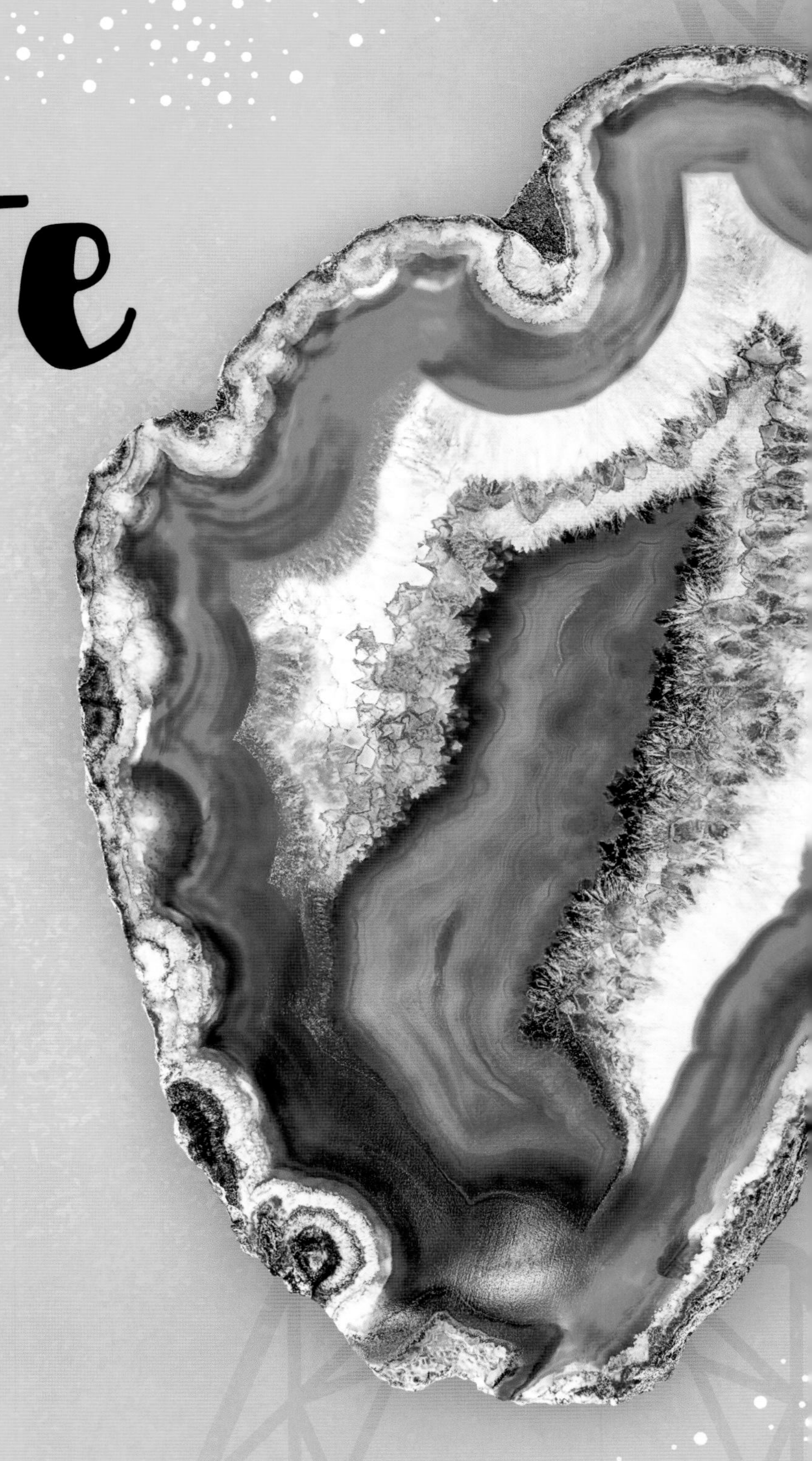

This stabilizing stone repels negative energy and remedies inner anger.

COLOR: **Varied**

Agate comes in a wide range of colors, including blue.

GOOD FOR:

Healing and grounding

Agate is treasured for creating balance and restoring yin and yang energies.

HARNESS THE POWER

Since ancient times, agate has been recognized for its protective properties. Persian magicians believed these stones were powerful enough to control thunder and lightning! Certain tribes in Brazil believe agate can heal scorpion stings as well as poisonous snakebites.

KEEP COOL

Besides making stunning jewelry, agate is a great one to pop on your desk to channel the positive vibes. It is used by people wanting to keep a cool head, while improving focus and concentration.

PATTERNS

If you look closely, you may spot some fascinating shapes within agate, from trees and plants to clouds or rivers, and even animals. These patterns are created by impurities present when it formed.

SPEAK YOUR TRUTH

If you're lost for words or feel like you're holding back from sharing how you really feel, then agate may allow you to open up. The ocean-toned blue agate is all about helping things flow. It's used to clear blocked throat chakras and empower you to be your authentic self.

CARING FOR AGATE

To keep agate fully charged and at its optimum, rinse it under running water for a quick and easy refresh and cleanse. The best care for this stone is to keep it out of sunlight.

Fluorite

Nicknamed the "genius stone," fluorite is believed to improve concentration and decision-making.

COLOR:

Varied

Fluorite comes in many different colors, including green.

GOOD FOR:

Headspace

Those seeking clarity may turn to this stone to dissolve brain fog.

NO BONES ABOUT IT

This colorful stone is a mineral made of calcium fluoride, so it's no wonder that it's the stone of choice for those with bone-related issues. Many believe in its power to relieve aching joints and tissues. It is also known as an antiviral stone that can be used to help flush infections out of the body.

GLOW FOR IT

If you place fluorite under UV (ultraviolet) light, it glows. That glow is what's known as fluorescence. In fact, the word "fluorescence" came from the word "fluorite" since this stone was among the first fluorescent specimens ever studied.

SUBTLE SHADES

Besides looking pretty, the various shades of fluorite have different benefits. For example, blue fluorite helps with rational thinking and improving communication. Purple fluorite is connected to the third eye chakra, which represents spiritual awareness, while green fluorite is perfect for those seeking higher meaning in life.

AND BREATHE...

If you're struggling to focus, take five minutes and meditate with fluorite nearby. It's an excellent stone for neutralizing negativity and eliminating stress. It's believed that placing this mineral around your home can help improve your attention span.

EVERYDAY FLUORITE

Fluorite is super versatile. Not only does it look beautiful in jewelry, but it's also an essential industrial mineral. Fluorite is used in aluminum and steel production, and it's present in everything from telescopes to camera lenses.

WHICH CRYSTAL DO YOU NEED?

With lots of crystals to choose from, it can be overwhelming to know which one is right for you. Use this handy guide as a starting point.

My friends would describe me as:

A. Thoughtful
B. Inquisitive
C. Funny
D. Quiet

At parties:

A. I want to make friends and have fun.
B. I'm wondering why I'm there.
C. I tend to make a fool out of myself.
D. I feel nervous and self-conscious.

My favorite color is:

A. Pink
B. Blue
C. Green
D. I can't pick!

I would rather spend my time:

A. In the city
B. In the woods
C. I don't mind, as long as it's far from danger!
D. Somewhere quiet, by water

My favorite subject is:

A. Drama
B. Psychology
C. Science
D. English

If I was an animal, I'd be a:

A. Dog
B. Cat
C. Monkey
D. Mouse

My favorite film genre is:

A. Romance
B. Thriller
C. Comedy
D. Drama

When it comes to homework:

A. I get it done early, so I have time to hang out with friends.
B. I tend to ask for help.
C. I often forget to do it, despite my best efforts to remember.
D. I worry that I've gotten the answers wrong.

Happiness to me is:

A. Friends and family
B. Knowing my purpose
C. Security
D. Freedom to be my authentic self

In group projects:

A. I like to be helpful.
B. I do my part and let someone else take the lead.
C. The work always falls on me.
D. I stay quiet and hope no one will notice me.

RESULTS:

Mostly As:
Rose Quartz
Your friend is rose quartz. You are kind and caring, and love being around people. Use this nurturing crystal to strengthen your current relationships and attract beautiful new ones.

Mostly Bs:
Lapis Lazuli
Your perfect match is lapis lazuli. You are a creative, deep thinker who often gets lost in their own thoughts. Use this enigmatic stone to put yourself on the path to enlightenment and find some answers.

Mostly Cs:
Jade
You need some jade—like, yesterday. Life has thrown some curve balls at you, and you could use a bit of luck! Use this generous crystal to attract good fortune and health.

Mostly Ds:
Topaz
You're going to want topaz. The world deserves to know the real you, and you deserve to feel confident in yourself. Use this powerful crystal to overcome anxiety and find your voice.

Pyrite

This dazzling stone has strong links to wealth, power, and protection.

COLOR:

Gold

Pyrite has a brassy yellow color and metallic luster.

GOOD FOR:

Fortune

Look to this stone for prosperity and protection from negative energy.

GO FOR IT

Use pyrite to light a fire in your belly and go after what you want. With its ability to increase strength, stamina, and leadership properties, you have all the ammunition you need to step up to your own potential.

BRIGHT SPARK

This stone takes its name from the Greek word for fire because of its fire-making abilities. When struck hard enough against metal or stone, it can create sparks—although we don't recommend trying this for yourself!

FOOL'S GOLD

In the old mining days, pyrite was often mistaken for gold and gained itself the nickname "fool's gold." Ironically, pyrite has little monetary value, but it is thought to bring fortune. Put it on display at home to increase your chances of attracting abundance.

LOOK THE PART

Pyrite also makes a great alternative to gold for jewelry. It is much more affordable than its counterpart but no less fashionable. Ancient Greeks used pyrite for the making of jewelry and amulets.

ONE-STONE-FITS-ALL

You can also use pyrite to better your health. This handy crystal is said to strengthen the circulatory and respiratory systems and protect against environmental pollutants. It can also be used to fight viral infections, reduce fevers, and strengthen the immune system.

Tourmaline

This stone is believed to boost creativity and encourage innovative ideas.

COLOR:

Varied

Tourmaline comes in many colors, from colorless to black, to everything in between.

GOOD FOR:

Creativity

If you are lacking inspiration or spirit, this stone is perfect for you.

RAINBOW STONE

Nicknamed the "rainbow stone," tourmaline has the widest color variety of any gemstone around. The different chemicals present in it create different hues. Its name even means "stone of mixed color" in Sinhalese (a language of Sri Lanka).

OPTICAL MAGIC

Tourmaline crystals are strongly dichroic. This means that its colors change depending on lighting conditions and the observer's viewing position. It is a very pretty stone that deserves to be shown off as jewelry.

PICK OF THE BARD

It is known as the gem of poets and creative artists. Throughout history, it has been worn by artists and writers to inspire creativity. It's even believed that Shakespeare had a small collection of tourmaline jewelry to help him overcome writer's block.

CHOICE OF CHAKRAS

The meanings associated with tourmaline vary depending on its color. Each color has its own chakra and unique healing abilities. Green and pink tourmaline (popular varieties of the crystal) are connected to the heart chakra and thought to promote healing, compassion, and forgiveness.

FEEL GREAT

There are physical benefits to this stone, too. It's widely believed tourmaline has the ability to remove toxins from the body and purify the blood. It's also thought to boost energy levels, reducing fatigue and promoting overall well-being.

Celestite

This calming stone helps encourage mental clarity and mindfulness.

COLOR:

Sky-blue

Celestite is commonly a delicate blue color, but other shades exist, including orange, green, and red.

GOOD FOR:

Mindfulness

Those feeling stressed or overwhelmed may benefit from celestite's calming properties.

BURN BRIGHT

Don't underestimate its power. Celestite might be soft, but it also packs a punch. The powdered form of it is actually used in fireworks because of its ability to burn with a bright red flame.

BYE-BYE STRESS

This crystal helps with stress and stress-related disorders. It is a good choice for those with digestion issues, as it's believed to reduce stomach pain and cramping. It's also thought to help reduce acne breakouts.

EASY DOES IT

Celestite is a very delicate gemstone and should be handled with care. Cleanse it by rinsing it with water or placing it in a bowl of salt. And while you do that, take a moment to be present and gentle with yourself.

PURE BLISS

Feeling frustrated or overwhelmed? This stone quiets the storm and helps people see clearly in moments of rage or stress. There's a reason why it takes its name from the Latin word for celestial—it's heavenly!

FREE TO BE ME

If you feel frequently misunderstood, celestite can help with that. Sky-blue celestite stimulates the throat chakra, which is the voice of the body. When this chakra is balanced, it is easier to communicate your thoughts and express yourself freely.

Azurite

A stone of intuition and inner strength, azurite is all about you.

COLOR:

Blue

Azurite ranges from light to dark blue, with medium-dark blue being the most common.

GOOD FOR:

Self-identity

This stone is thought to break through emotional blockages and bring harmony to its user.

PIECE OF HEAVEN

In China, azurite was nicknamed the "stone of heaven" for its perceived ability to open celestial gateways. It was similarly revered by Indigenous Americans who used it to communicate with spirit guides, and by ancient Greeks and Romans who valued its visionary insights and healing powers.

WORK OF ART

The name azurite comes from the stone's beautiful azure blue color, which was used as pigment in paint for centuries. In fact, azurite is said to be the most important blue pigment in European painting from the 15th–17th century.

GOOD VIBRATIONS

To experience azurite's insightful powers for yourself, wear it close to your skin and let those high vibrations get to work. Don't forget to charge it too—under starlight works best!

AZURITE AND ATHENA

Azurite has some strong, sage associations. It is connected to the third eye chakra, which is the center of intuition; and in Greek mythology, it is associated with Athena, the goddess of wisdom.

ATLANTIS

Legend has it, azurite originated in the lost, mythical city of Atlantis—a utopian island that was swallowed by the sea. This connection shrouds the stone in mystery and only adds to its magic.

MEDITATING WITH CRYSTALS

As you've seen by now, crystals have been used in healing practices for centuries—some sources estimate as far back as 6,000 years ago! There are many therapeutic ways to use your crystals; one popular choice is to meditate with them.

WHY USE CRYSTALS TO MEDITATE?

Meditating with crystals is thought to be beneficial for several reasons. For a start, it reinforces intentions. By asking yourself what you want out of meditating and choosing a crystal that corresponds with it, you are more likely to manifest a successful outcome. Crystals can also help raise your consciousness and lead to a more enriching meditation practice.

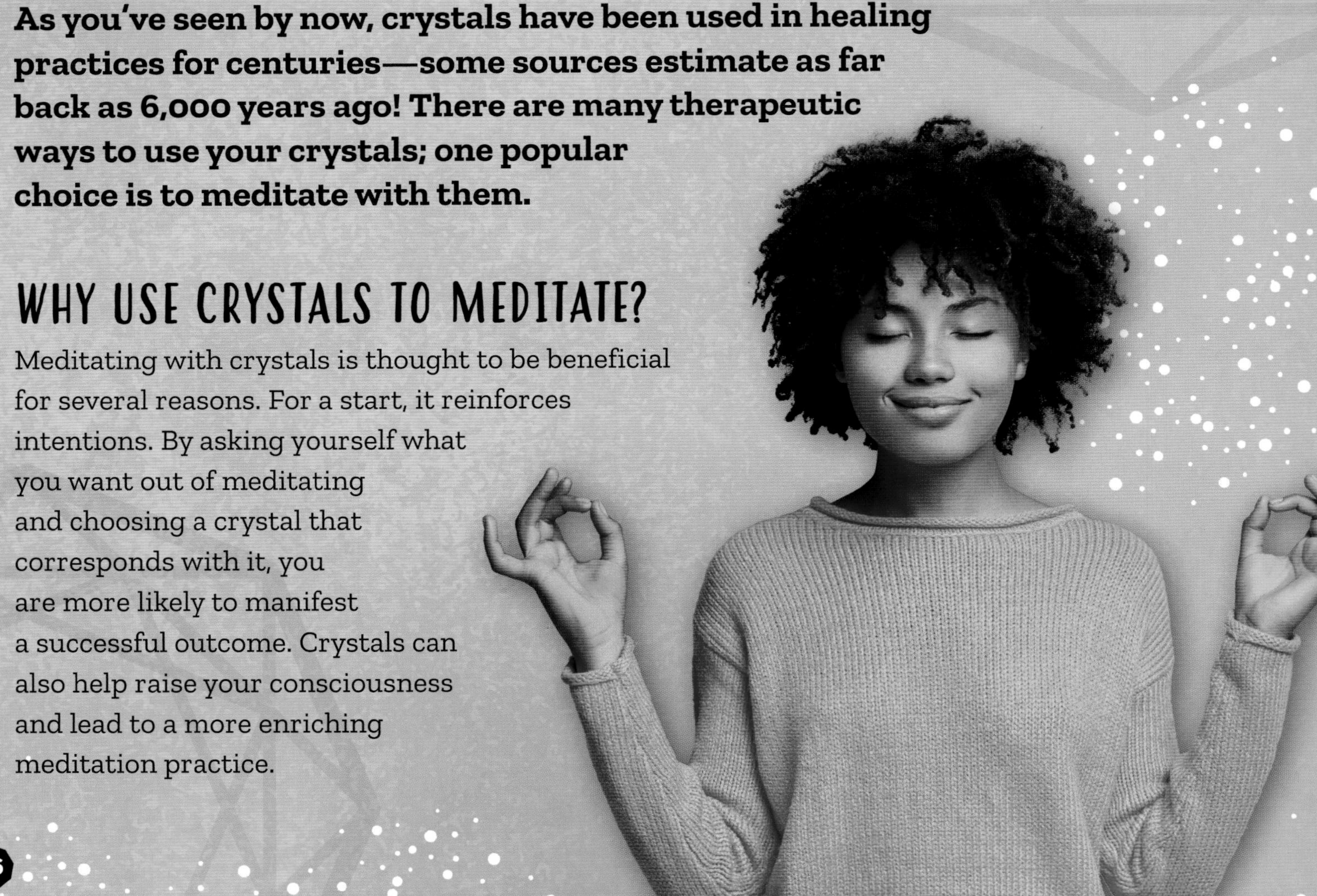

HOW TO MEDITATE WITH CRYSTALS:

Now you know why to meditate with crystals, here's a step-by-step of how to.

1. **Set your intentions.** Ask yourself what outcome you are seeking. For example, are you hoping to dispel negativity? Or is it spiritual growth you are after?

2. **Choose the best crystal for the job.** Each crystal has a different purpose, and some are better at one thing than another. Pick the right one for you, and don't forget to cleanse it beforehand.

3. **Ask the crystal for permission.** Connect with your crystal by asking to use its energy during the meditation.

4. **Meditate.** Now for the main show: hold the crystal in your hands, close your eyes, clear your mind, and relax. You might want to put the crystal on different areas of your body corresponding with the different chakras. For example, to stimulate the third eye chakra, hold the crystal against your forehead, in between your brows.

5. **Thank the crystal for its use.** If you are feeling particularly grateful, why not thank the crystal for its use? It's good practice to spread positivity and, as the saying goes, what goes around comes around!

POPULAR CRYSTALS TO MEDITATE WITH:

You can meditate with any crystal you want, but some popular choices are:

AMETHYST

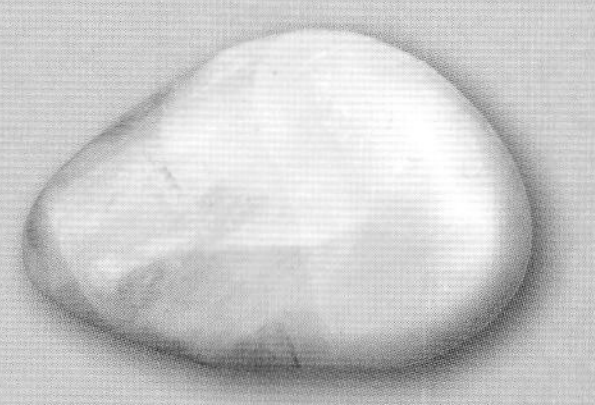

ROSE QUARTZ

CITRINE

LAPIS LAZULI

Ruby

This dazzling stone ignites love and protects its wearer.

COLOR:

Red

Ruby comes in many shades of red, the most common being vibrant red to slightly purplish.

GOOD FOR:

The heart

Promoting power, passion, and protection, this stone is pretty perfect.

RED HOT

With its fiery red color, it's unsurprising that ruby is associated with the Sun. Ancient Hindus, for one, believed ruby symbolized the Sun and could bring success, wealth, and power to its user. Their name for the stone, "Rajnapura," means "king of gems" in English.

LOVE IS IN THE AIR

Ruby symbolizes love and romance, and rubies are often chosen as gifts for 15th and 40th wedding anniversaries. It is one of the four precious gemstones besides emerald, sapphire, and diamond.

HEALING HEARTS

Ruby can also heal your heart in a physical sense. It is thought to strengthen the heart, muscles, and ventricles, and improve blood circulation. If this sounds good to you, wear it as a necklace and keep it close to the chest, where it can work its magic.

STRONG PROTECTOR

Did you know rubies are extremely strong? In fact, they are the second strongest gemstone after diamonds. That's good news for a stone that's all about protection!

WARM HUG

This stone is believed to stimulate the root and heart chakra, promoting a sense of security and compassion. It is a good choice for those nursing a wounded or broken heart because it can help restore trust in yourself and others.

Emerald

A stone of growth and love, emerald fortifies the spirit and promotes friendship.

COLOR:

Green

Emerald is typically bluish-green to pure green in color.

GOOD FOR:

Deepening bonds

Those wishing to strengthen their relationships may find a friend in emerald.

BE REBORN

Emerald gets its name from the Sanskrit word "Marakata," meaning the green of growing things. It's a fitting description of the stone, which has long been associated with vitality and rebirth.

MYSTIC VISIONS

According to legend, placing an emerald under the tongue would allow a person to see into the future. Additionally, wearing the stone could help decipher if a lover's promise was true or not and make the wearer an eloquent speaker.

MAGIC MOMENTS

In the past, magicians used emerald to receive visions. They would use it to leave their physical bodies and interpret signs being sent to them, knowing they would be protected from harm.

FEEL REJUVENATED

Packed with rejuvenating energy, emerald is great for the body. Aristotle was a great fan of the gemstone, believing it could soothe the eyes and help ward off the "falling sickness." But beyond that, emerald is thought to alleviate headaches, sharpen memory, and promote circulatory and neurological function.

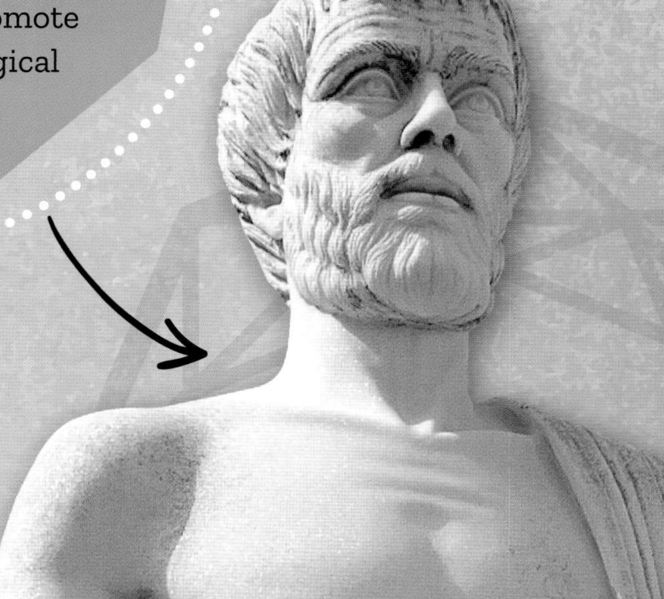

LET THE LOVE IN

Connected to the heart chakra, emerald heals emotional blockages to let in love and compassion. It can show you how to be a kinder, gentler person and improve relationships.

Labradorite

A highly mystical and magical stone, Labradorite is thought to strengthen intuition and offer a connection to the universe.

PSYCHIC POWERS

Connected to the third eye chakra, Labradorite strengthens intuition and offers a window to the spiritual world. It is also thought to enhance psychic abilities, such as clairvoyance and telepathic communication.

COLOR: **Varied**

Labradorite is an iridescent stone, meaning its colors—which can include blue, green, yellow, orange, and red—seem to change when seen from different angles.

GOOD FOR: **Spiritual growth**

This stone is thought to raise consciousness and promote psychic abilities.

MIRACLE WORKER

Ancient Inuits called labradorite a "fire stone" and would use powdered forms of it to help cure ailments. Still today, labradorite is thought to support respiratory health, aid in digestion, and relieve anxiety and stress.

MOONLIGHT MAGIC

To clean labradorite, rinse it under running water and scrub gently with a soft cloth. This will help clear the stone of negative energy and keep it in good shape. To give it an energetic reset, leave it out overnight to absorb the Moon's magical rays.

OPTICAL ILLUSION

Labradorite is well known for being iridescent, meaning its bright colors change with movement and in different lighting conditions. In relation to the stone, this optical phenomenon is known as labradorescence.

AURORA BOREALIS

With its luminous colors, labradorite has associations with the northern lights and is nicknamed "the aurora borealis stone." Ancient Inuits even believed labradorite was the fallen rays from the auroras captured in a stone.

Aragonite

A stabilizing stone, aragonite encourages truth and understanding.

COLOR:

Orange

Aragonite typically comes in varying hues of red, orange, and yellow. It can be other colors, such as green and gray.

GOOD FOR:

Emotional Stability

Those feeling stressed or overwhelmed may look to aragonite for grounding.

TAKE CARE

Take extra care with aragonite—it is a soft crystal and therefore more prone to damage. Clean it with lukewarm water and a soft cloth and charge it in gentle sunlight. Alternatively, bury it in soil and let Mother Nature do her thing.

TWO FOR ONE

Aragonite has the same chemical structure as calcite and has the potential to share its healing properties, too. Over time, aragonite will become calcite if left, which is just one of the wonderful things about this crystal!

This crystal is thought to be connected to the mystical earth star chakra. Located below the feet, this chakra serves as an extension of the root chakra, providing a deeper connection to Mother Earth.

FEEL WARM INSIDE

Feeling cold? Aragonite can help with that, too. This nurturing stone can combat chills and warm up the extremities. It's also thought to ease stress-related problems, such as poor sleep and tension headaches.

AND RELAX...

With its ability to induce peace and calm, aragonite is an excellent stone to meditate with. Sit with it in your palms and let its comforting energy flow through you.

CRYSTALS AT HOME

So you've got your first crystals, but how do you optimize their powers? Here are some tips on how to use your crystals at home, from the best ways to display them to the best ways to care for them!

DISPLAYING YOUR CRYSTALS

At the entrance

When it comes to placing stones somewhere to ward off negative energy, the hallway near to the door is the perfect spot. Tourmaline in the entrance to your home can be used to stop negative energy getting into the house.

On the mat

Bring your crystals along for yoga practice or meditation. Simply roll out your mat and place the stones nearby to help you tune into your inner calm.

In the living room

When it comes to making a feature of your crystals, the mantelpiece is a central spot to show them off and appreciate their beauty.

While you work or study

To inspire creativity and focus, putting crystals on your desk is a good place to start. Look for crystals that clear brain fog and help motivate you.

In the bathroom

Soak up the benefits of your crystal by bathing with them. We all know a warm bath is a great way to de-stress and unwind after a long day, so imagine adding crystals into the mix! Many stones and crystals are happy to be submerged but always check your specific crystal is compatible with water first. If not, the edge of the bath does the trick, too!

In the bedroom

Try placing calming crystals on your bedside table to encourage good quality sleep and rest. They also look cute arranged in a ring dish or jewelry holder. Amethyst is great for calming the mind and can promote better sleep.

Close at hand

Don't forget to hold them in your palms during those times you need support for a particularly tricky moment.

Among your plants

Plant pots make a great home to nestle crystals in. If they're not water-safe, just be sure to remove them before you water your plants.

CRYSTAL GRIDS

You may choose to display crystals in grids, which is a way of arranging them in geometric shapes or patterns. Grids combine the energies from different stones and can be used for healing and manifesting abundance. Arranging them like this is believed to maximize the power of crystals.

CARING FOR CRYSTALS . . .

1. Extreme temperatures and humidity can negatively affect crystals. The best way to store them is in a dry, dark place—be sure to avoid direct sunlight.
2. If you store them together, it's wise to wrap them in soft fabric to prevent them from scratching one another.
3. Recharge crystals outside around every month or so. Just put them out on your windowsill overnight during a full moon.
4. To cleanse crystals, bury them in soil overnight to get rid of toxins and negative energy that has built up over time.

Malachite

This transformative stone empowers individuals to face their fears and fulfill their potential.

COLOR:

Green

Malachite is an opulent, deep green color.

GOOD FOR:

Change

This stone is great for inviting positive change and welcoming growth.

ANCIENT TIMES

Malachite has long been considered a guardian of the heart, so it's no wonder many wear the stone as jewelry. And it's no new thing! Ancient Egyptians mined malachite back in 4000 BC and were quick to adorn themselves in jewelry containing the beautiful gemstone. They also ground it down into pigment to create Cleopatra-esque eye shadow.

MALACHITE ROOM

The Malachite Room of the Winter Palace in St. Petersburg, Russia, is brimming with over 200 tons of malachite. When it's carved into, the stone's striking swirls and patterns are revealed, which is why it's so popular in sculpture.

FOR HEALING

If you suffer with a phobia that is holding you back, it may be worth giving this green gem a try. Malachite can help overcome fears as well as with anxiety more generally, freeing people up to move forward. The super calming stone is also thought to keep blood pressure low and reduce physical symptoms of anxiety.

PROTECTION

In the Middle Ages, malachite was worn as a sun-shaped pendant for protection against bad health and depression. It was also considered invaluable in tackling ailments relating to the stomach.

WARDING OFF EVIL

If you're looking for a stone to make you feel safe and taken care of, malachite can do just that. Ancient Egyptians, Greeks, and Romans swore by its power to keep evil spirits at bay. It often featured in jewelry and small ornaments.

Chrysocolla

Open up channels of communication so that you can speak your truth with chrysocolla.

COLOR:

Blue-green

Chrysocolla ranges from blue to green in color.

GOOD FOR:

Communication

If you've got to make a speech or share your knowledge, then this stone could be just what you need.

INSPIRES CREATIVITY

For centuries, chrysocolla has inspired creativity. Its name comes from the Greek word "chrysos," which translates as gold and "kola," which means glue. In ancient Roman times, goldsmiths used the rock as solder to weld pieces together. Renaissance painters also made use of chrysocolla and would grind it down to make pigment for paint.

COOL DOWN

Ancient Egyptians called chrysocolla the "wise stone," and it was a favorite for negotiations. Cleopatra famously loved chrysocolla and carried it with her everywhere she went. Among its uses, it was believed to act as a shield, stimulate the mind, and encourage sensitivity.

SUPER SOOTHING

Calling all worriers out there! This stone is thought to support and soothe the nervous system. Some even believe that having this stone nearby can lower blood pressure by reducing anxiety and depression.

THE TEACHING STONE

Chrysocolla is known as the "teaching stone" because it enables communication, knowledge, and transformation. Hold this stone close for speeches or public speaking as it is connected to the throat chakra for communication, and the heart chakra for compassion when interacting with others.

POWER UP

To enhance the impact of chrysocolla, you can pair it with its cousin crystals of malachite and blue azurite. This combination will amplify the stones' effects on your body, allowing for greater self-understanding and communication.

Rhodochrosite

Related to self-love, forgiveness, and compassion, rhodochrosite invites us to care for ourselves as well as those around us.

COLOR:

Pink

This rosy-toned stone invites both self-love and selfless love.

GOOD FOR:

Meditation

Enhance meditative practice and spiritual work by introducing this stone.

SELFLESS LOVE

Rhodochrosite is the symbol of selfless love and going above and beyond for others, but it's also about personal growth. It's known for encouraging self-love and taking care of old wounds. You may have feelings that you've buried from the past—this stone helps you look deeper into those in order to learn from them.

REUNITE

Some believe this stone and its focus on compassion can help reunite people with long-lost family or friends. To encourage this, people must put their rhodochrosite near a photo of a loved one. When it comes to a missing pet, just leave the stone in the pet's favorite spot and imagine the animal back there.

SEEKING HAPPINESS

If you ever feel like you're a bit of a lone wolf, wearing this stone can guide you toward a new soulmate and valuable connection. It's believed to lead you toward emotional happiness, inviting you to be vulnerable without the fear of rejection.

MOTHER EARTH

Rhodochrosite is an earth stone, so it's all about celebrating the wonder of nature. What's more, it's about recognizing and being grateful for the responsibility we share to care for Mother Earth. Rhodochrosite invites us to help it heal.

LIVE IN THE NOW

Creativity and spontaneity are maximized with this stone nearby. It can be all too easy to put something off for another day, but rhodochrosite can be a motivator to get up and go and helps tackle procrastination.

Topaz

Allow the wisdom of topaz to guide you down the right path.

COLOR:

Varied

Topaz can be a variety of colors, including orange and blue.

GOOD FOR:

Confidence

If you tend to shy away from putting yourself out there, topaz offers a big dose of courage.

PERFECT PEACE

In mythology, topaz is a gem of peace and healing. It was first found more than two millennia ago by the Romans who discovered it on an island called Topazios in the Red Sea. It was believed it could protect its wearer from enemies as well as resolve lingering disagreements.

KEEP COOL

For those who often feel overwhelmed or flustered, topaz is a go-to! It's all about keeping cool no matter what. The stone itself has a unique ability to cool down quickly after being in hot environments, which is why it's known as the "cooling stone."

Taylor Swift and Katy Perry have been spotted wearing topaz.

AUTHENTICITY

Known as the stone of clarity, topaz is all about embracing your authentic self. It encourages you to channel the wisdom within and guides you down the right pathways.

SUPER SOOTHER

Many turn to topaz for issues involving the throat or head. This cooling blue beauty soothes a sore throat and can banish unwanted stress and jaw clenching. Better still, it is also thought to relieve migraine pressure.

SHINE BRIGHT

Those with a fear of public speaking may find this gem amplifies their voice. Topaz empowers people who usually play it safe to reach for the stars. By doing so, they are open to the opportunities to meet their full potential.

OTHER USES FOR CRYSTALS

As you've seen, there are many ways to use your crystals. From infusing your water to protecting yourself against electromagnetic frequencies, here are some fun options you might've missed, plus a run-down of how some celebs like to use theirs!

WHY NOT...

Make a crystal elixir

A crystal elixir is a fancy name for water infused with crystals. Some people make a crystal elixir by actually putting the crystal in the water, but you should never do this, as some crystals could be toxic! Instead, leave your crystal next to a fresh water bottle overnight, to infuse it with energy.

Add them into your beauty routine

Rose quartz and jade have been used for centuries to rejuvenate the skin and help it stay firm. Nowadays, they are typically sold as face rollers and Gua Sha—a smooth-edged tool to massage the skin. Beauty gurus rave about them, and they're gorgeous too!

Make them into jewelry

Sure, you can buy crystal jewelry, but wouldn't it be so much fun to make some yourself? It might sound difficult, but it doesn't have to be. There are plenty of easy tutorials to follow online.

Use them as a paperweight

Why use a boring old paperweight when you can use a crystal instead? They get the job done and look pretty doing it. Plus, there's a double benefit to this. Having the crystal near you while you work = absorbing its uplifting energy!

Place them under your pillow

We've spoken about placing crystals on your bedside table to promote good sleep, but why not take it one step further and place them under your pillow? Keeping them close is thought to increase their calming and protective energy.

Use them as a cleansing tool

You know how to cleanse crystals, but do you know they can be used for cleansing themselves? Some crystals, including clear quartz, have self-cleaning abilities and can be used to purify other crystals. Simply have the self-cleaning crystal touch the other crystal(s) and let it do its thing.

Put them in your purse

Whatever you're hoping to attract—love, wealth, happiness—carrying a crystal with you is never a bad idea.

HOW CELEBS USE THEIR CRYSTALS...

Miranda Kerr is obsessed with crystals and uses them in everything from meditation to her skincare line.

Katy Perry once said she carries rose quartz to attract love!

Jenna Dewan has an entire YouTube video dedicated to how she uses her crystals, which includes putting them in her purse and bath.

Adele uses crystals to combat stage fright.

Victoria Beckham puts crystals by her bed to sleep well.

Kim Kardashian loves wearing crystals and famously wore an outfit made almost entirely of Swarovski crystals.

RECORD-BREAKING CRYSTALS

Every crystal is unique, but these five really stand out. From a $71.2 million diamond to a 26-feet-wide geode, these crystals are a cut above the rest!

Most EXPENSIVE CRYSTAL Ever Sold

The Pink Star is an incredibly rare pink diamond that sold at auction for a whopping $71.2 million in 2017. Bought by Hong Kong jewelry company Chow Tai Fook, the diamond is graded as internally flawless and weighs 59.60 carats. It originated from a 132.5-carat rough and was cut and polished over a period of two years.

World's RAREST Gemstone

Found almost exlusively in Sri Lanka and Tanzania, Taaffeite is considered the rarest gemstone on Earth. The stunning stone, which comes in shades of pink and purple, as well as other less-common color varieties, was discovered by Richard Taaffe in October 1945. For many years after Taaffe's discovery, few samples were found. Even now, there are under 50 known samples in the world.

World's LARGEST Crystals

The Cave of the Crystals in Mexico has some of the largest crystals in the world. Buried 1,000 feet beneath the Sierra de Naica mountain, these selenite crystals are at least half a million years old. Many are 13 to 20 feet in length, and the very largest is 36 feet tall. Some of the heaviest crystals are estimated to weigh up to 55 tons.

World's LARGEST GEODE

A geode is a cavity inside a rock that is lined with crystals. Pulpí Geode is one of the largest crystal "caves" ever found and the largest geode in the world, measuring 26 feet wide, 6.5 feet high, and 6.5 feet deep. It was found inside an abandoned silver mine in Southern Spain in 1999 and was opened to the public in 2019.

LARGEST Known Crystal CLUSTER

The world's largest quartz crystal cluster weighs around 15 tons and measures 10 feet wide, and 10 feet high. It was discovered in 1985 at the bottom of a 150-foot-deep cave in the Otjua Mine in Namibia and took five years to excavate. It is currently on display at Kristall Galerie, a gemstone museum in Swakopmund, Namibia.

CRYSTALS AT A GLANCE

Malachite

Emerald

Jade

Fluorite

Calcite

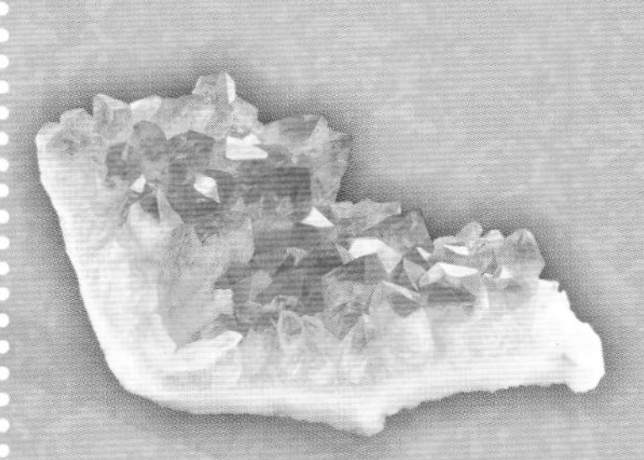

Citrine

Aragonite

Apophyllite

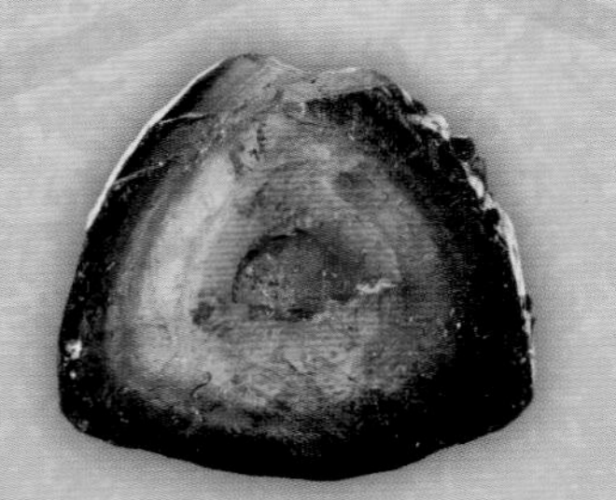

Tourmaline

Ruby

Rhodonite

Rose Quartz